DATE DUE

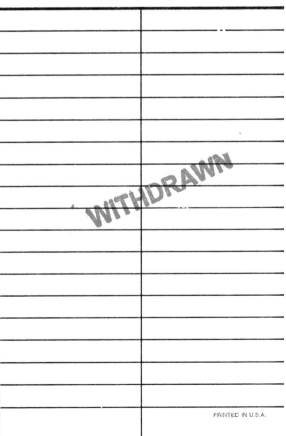

PRINTED IN U.S.A.

essential careers

CAREERS IN
HEATING, VENTILATION, AND AIR-CONDITIONING (HVAC)

LINDA BICKERSTAFF

ROSEN
PUBLISHING

NEW YORK

Published in 2014 by The Rosen Publishing Group, Inc.
29 East 21st Street, New York, NY 10010

Library of Congress Cataloging-in-Publication Data

Bickerstaff, Linda.
Careers in heating, ventilation, and air conditioning (HVAC) / Linda Bickerstaff.—
First edition.
    pages cm.—(Essential careers)
Includes bibliographical references and index.
ISBN 978-1-4488-9478-9 (library binding)
1. Heating and ventilation industry—Vocational guidance. 2. Air conditioning industry—Vocational guidance. I. Title.
HD9683.A2B53 2013
697.0023—dc23

                                                                    2012039554

Manufactured in the United States of America

CPSIA Compliance Information: Batch #S13YA: For further information, contact Rosen Publishing, New York, New York, at 1-800-237-9932.

contents

This HVAC technician was very popular during a summer heat wave in New Mexico. He quickly repaired this air conditioner and left the homeowners basking in its cool breeze.

DUCTION

Fats Domino (1928–) is a rhythm and blues singer and pianist from New Orleans, Louisiana, and a member of the Rock and Roll Hall of Fame. He once said, "A lot of fellows nowadays have a B.A., M.D., or Ph.D. Unfortunately they don't have a J.O.B." During the recent economic downturn, many people found themselves in the same situation. Those with solid careers in the heating, ventilation, and air-conditioning (HVAC) industry, however, seem to have weathered the economic crisis well.

Does the following job advertisement for the HVAC industry sound too good to be true?

> Wanted! Creative high school graduates with good "people skills" who enjoy making and repairing things. One hundred thousand jobs are available in an economically stable industry. Excellent salaries, good job security, and almost unlimited possibilities for advancement are guaranteed. Applicants must be self-starters who are able to make independent decisions while working well with others.

Well, it isn't! This industry was not as devastated in the economic downturn that began in 2008. Although a few of the less skilled workers in the industry lost their jobs, most not only kept working, but also made advancements in their careers. Now that the economy is recovering, the HVAC industry is ready to explosively expand into new and exciting areas of service. It is limited, however, by an inadequate number of trained workers to carry the industry into the future. The U.S. Bureau of Labor Statistics (BLS) says that one hundred thousand workers are needed *right now* to replace retiring workers and to fill the expanding needs of this growth industry.

What do people in the HVAC industry do? The majority of them install, maintain, and repair heating and air-conditioning systems in homes, schools, office buildings, hospitals, shopping malls, and all the other facilities in which good climate control is necessary. HVAC installers and mechanics, collectively called technicians, are the backbone of the industry. They take equipment designed and made by others, modify it for a particular job, put it where it needs to be, and make it work.

With experience and continuing education, technicians often become supervisors or open their own HVAC businesses. Others, with specialized computer skills, design HVAC systems. Some HVAC technicians work in refrigeration services, a specialized part of the industry. These services are critical to food processing and storage companies. Refrigeration is also important in some chemical companies and in high-tech companies whose equipment must be kept cool to function properly.

Pursuing a career in the HVAC industry offers much more than just a job—a piece of work for which one is paid. It offers the satisfaction of knowing that the work benefits the health and comfort of everyone. It is necessary here on Earth and is absolutely critical if people are to explore the depths of the oceans and the vastness of space. It is a career that is "going green," is in need of well-trained, enthusiastic workers, and is waiting for you!

chapter 1

CAREER CHOICES IN THE HVAC INDUSTRY

There are many job titles within the HVAC industry. The people holding these jobs are concerned with climate-control systems that keep people warm in the winter, cool in the summer, and breathing the freshest air possible all year long. People who get satisfaction from working with their hands in the process of solving problems are likely to find a satisfying and challenging job in this industry.

HVAC JOB TITLES

The following are a few of the job titles held by people working in the HVAC industry:

HVAC installers and HVAC mechanics are entry-level workers. Almost all mechanics are also trained as installers. A person with training in both areas is called a technician. Technicians make up the bulk of the HVAC workforce. They must be able to read blueprints to aid in installing furnaces, heat pumps, and air-conditioning units. They also install the ductwork that carries treated air, make all electrical connections, and install thermostats. They must also be able to provide maintenance for the equipment they install. This servicing may include, among other things, cleaning fans, installing new filters, oiling parts, and adjusting thermostats so that HVAC systems work more efficiently.

Repair technicians usually have more training than installers or mechanics. They must be able to diagnose problems that

Newly designed and manufactured Trane HVAC equipment must pass extreme environmental tests before it is sold. This Trane engineer monitors equipment undergoing the Systems Extreme Environmental Test (SEET) at the company's lab.

arise in HVAC equipment. Once they find the problems, they must be able to make appropriate repairs. Repair technicians must have excellent "people skills" because equipment failures frequently lead to unhappy customers. They also benefit from being good salespeople. If malfunctioning equipment can't be repaired, it has to be replaced. They must be able to give information about new equipment options to home or business owners. Repair technicians should also be able to provide information on the service or maintenance contracts offered by their companies. HVAC equipment that is inspected and maintained on a regular basis by a HVAC technician works more efficiently and lasts longer.

Master technicians have several years of experience and advanced certifications. They often supervise other technicians and may become foremen or project supervisors in companies employing many technicians.

HVAC drafters may or may not be trained as HVAC technicians. Their jobs involve making drawings or pictures of HVAC systems. Today, these drawings are made using computer software designed specifically for the HVAC industry. Most HVAC drafters have associate's degrees in drafting, and many have bachelor's degrees in architecture or engineering. They all have excellent computer skills. They work with mechanical engineers and design engineers to create the plans for the HVAC equipment needed in various construction jobs.

HVAC design engineers design HVAC systems for new construction and figure out how to fit replacement units into older buildings. They're especially concerned with seeing that HVAC designs address environmental issues. Most design engineers have bachelor's degrees in HVAC technology, mechanical engineering, or architectural engineering.

HVAC engineers are mechanical engineers with special interests in HVAC systems. They work with architects in the development of blueprints and do much of the initial planning on what types of equipment to install for each job. They manage labor and operating costs and are generally "the HVAC boss" on major construction projects.

Refrigeration maintenance technicians specialize in operating and maintaining industrial refrigeration systems. They may be HVAC technicians with additional training in refrigeration, or they may have specifically trained for a career in refrigeration alone. They are able to adjust and repair a variety of refrigeration system components. They must pass examinations given by the U.S. Environmental Protection Agency (EPA) to certify that they know the proper ways to work with or dispose of refrigerant gases. Many are employed in food and beverage processing plants and in cold storage facilities. Others work for those who make and/or install refrigeration systems.

WHAT ABOUT THE "V" IN HVAC?

The letter "V" stands for "ventilation." Although it may seem that ventilation is not as important as the heating and cooling aspects of climate-control systems, nothing could be further from the truth. Improperly ventilated systems don't function

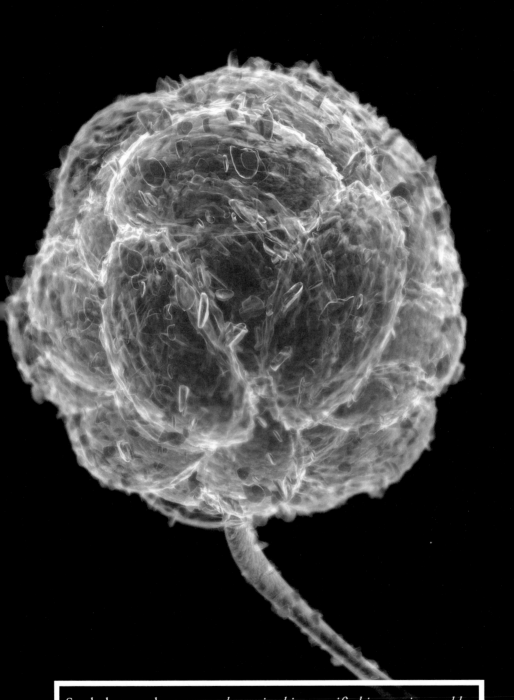

Stachybotrys chartarum, *shown in this magnified image, is a mold found in moist areas in many homes. Its spores can be quite toxic and are implicated in "sick building syndrome."*

SEVEN MILLION AMERICAN CHILDREN HAVE ASTHMA

In May 2012, the EPA issued a news release saying that more than seven million children in the United States suffer from asthma, a lung disorder that children may or may not outgrow as they get older. It also said that the economic cost of asthma amounts to $56 billion each year. This includes direct medical costs from hospital stays and indirect costs such as lost school days for children or lost workdays for adults with asthma. An article from the National Center for Healthy Housing expanded on this report. It said that over the last thirty years, the number of cases of asthma has doubled in the general population and increased fourfold among low-income families. Major causes of this increase are inadequate ventilation in homes and the presence of mold and mildew in climate-control systems. Molds and mildew often serve as triggers for asthma attacks.

efficiently and can even be deadly. In recent years, the issue of indoor air quality has become progressively more important. Elisabeth Leamy, a journalist who writes consumer stories for ABC News, says the EPA considers indoor air quality to be the fourth-greatest pollution threat to Americans.

Inadequate ventilation is thought to contribute to the outbreak of infectious epidemics such as those reported on cruise ships and at conventions, where large numbers of people congregate in small, confined spaces. It's also associated with a condition called "sick building syndrome" in which people, upon entering a building, suddenly feel ill or uncomfortable.

After they leave the building, they quickly recover. No specific cause has been found for the symptoms that people experience. The EPA also reports that indoor air pollution is one cause for the increased incidence of asthma, a common lung disorder, among Americans, especially young people.

HVAC technicians are on the front line in the fight against indoor air pollution. They are responsible for the maintenance of ventilation systems that are associated with climate-control units. This aspect of their jobs has become even more important because many of the buildings being constructed today have no windows that can be opened to allow fresh outdoor air to enter. Well-maintained ventilation systems are essential to the quality of life for everyone. They are life itself for those who travel in airliners or spaceships and those who will someday live in hostile environments such as undersea cities or colonies on the moon.

chapter 2

Is a Career in HVAC Right for You?

Marshall Brain, founder of HowStuffWorks.com, says in his book *The Teenager's Guide to the Real World*, "For many teenagers, one of the hardest questions to answer is 'What do you want to be when you grow up?'" Most teens have trouble answering that question. They have thought about many possible careers but haven't found the one that's just right for them. How do people decide what they want to do? More specifically, how does a teen decide if a career in HVAC will be a good choice?

The first step is to consider the personality traits of people who are happy in their HVAC careers. The second step is to get as much information about the HVAC industry as possible. The third step is to choose high school classes that will introduce some of the basic skills needed in the industry.

PERSONALITY TYPES: WHAT ARE THEY, AND HOW ARE THEY USED?

Carl Jung (1875–1961), a Swiss psychiatrist (a doctor who studies the human mind), was the first person to talk about personality types. His work, and that done by many others, was used to develop a set of personality traits common to people in particular jobs. Career counselors frequently use this information to guide teens toward careers for which they are well suited.

An HVAC installer puts in an air filtration system called CleanEffects, which can remove 99.98 percent of airborne allergens from the air. It is 100 times more effective than regular room air filters.

Dr. Laurence Shatkin, a noted expert on careers and occupations, in his book *Best Jobs for the 21st Century* says there are six personality types, each with a set of fundamental characteristics. The six types listed by Shatkin are: realistic personalities; investigative personalities; artistic personalities; social personalities; enterprising personalities; and conventional personalities. Most people in the HVAC industry fall into the realistic personality group. They are practical people who like to work with their hands. They enjoy working with tools and machinery and often prefer outdoor jobs. They also enjoy solving problems. They are easy-going people who prefer working alone or in small groups. They are usually very self-confident.

Personality traits have been used to develop quizzes to be taken by people who are investigating different career choices. Five of the questions from the HVAC Technician Quiz, found at CareerPlanning.About.com, are:

1. Are you good at working with your hands?
2. Are you willing to work with potentially dangerous equipment and under dangerous conditions?
3. Is your body flexible?
4. Which do you prefer, a desk job or a job that requires you to be physically active?
5. Are you honest?

Most HVAC technicians agree that they have all or most of the personality traits listed in Shatkin's realistic group. They also have many skills in common. In a forum conducted by Indeed.com, HVAC technicians were asked what they believe to be the top three nontechnical skills that every HVAC technician needs to excel in his or her career. One responder said that a technician must have drive, determination, and self-discipline, as well as good communication skills.

Sources of Information About the HVAC Industry

Gathering information about careers in the HVAC industry is the next step. The BLS has a wealth of information in its *Occupational Outlook Handbook* (http://www.bls.gov/ooh). There are also numerous articles on the Web and in career books about what HVAC technicians do. The best source of information, however, comes from the industry itself. In an attempt to attract young people to HVAC careers, several companies sponsor career days in middle schools and high schools.

Seaman's Air Conditioning and Refrigeration, Inc., is one company that is actively taking HVAC to students. At career days for ninth-grade students in Kentwood, Michigan, public schools, technicians from Seaman's set up several interactive stations that demonstrate heating, welding, sheet metal work,

To promote the industry to potential employees, HVAC equipment parts manufacturers such as the Tianjin Pipe Company sponsor career days for high school and college students.

air flow measurements, refrigeration theory, applied refrigeration, and an ice machine. Technicians at each station make many presentations to students who visit the various sites throughout the day. Jeff Block, one of Seaman's representatives who works at career days, says, "Our industry has changed so much in such a short time that the kids really need to know about the opportunities we offer for them to work with technology and electronics." Students attending career days also receive handouts listing jobs and their descriptions, salary ranges, and other pertinent information about careers in HVAC.

The American Society of Heating, Refrigeration and Air-Conditioning Engineers (ASHRAE) is also a good source of information about the HVAC industry. It focuses on, through its participation in the STEM (Science, Technology, Engineering, and Math) Education Coalition, attracting kids in Generation Y to engineering careers in the HVAC industry. Generation Y is composed of young people born between 1984 and 2002. ASHRAE publishes posters and brochures and has developed videos about the industry that are fun and informative. Members of the society visit middle school classrooms to talk about the industry, its need for new young engineers, and the importance of the HVAC industry in sustaining and improving the world in which they live.

JUMP-START AN HVAC CAREER IN HIGH SCHOOL

High schools have core curricula taken by all students. These courses of study usually include four years of English and three years each of mathematics, science, and social studies. Most high schools also offer courses in technical skills such as typing, computer science, and the industrial arts. Subjects studied in industrial arts classes include auto-mechanics, welding, and

SkillsUSA Helps Ensure a Skilled Workforce for America

In 1965, two hundred students, advisers, and leaders from business and labor organizations met to form the Vocational Industrial Clubs of America. In 2004, it changed its name to SkillsUSA. It now has more than seventeen thousand chapters in fifty-four states and territories. Over the years, it has served more than 10.5 million members. About three hundred thousand students and advisers join each year. The goal of the organization is to ensure that America has a skilled workforce by helping students prepare for careers in technical and service occupations.

According to information from its Web site, "SkillsUSA programs include local, state, and national competitions in which students demonstrate occupational and leadership skills." Each year, a national contest is held in which more than 5,600 students compete in ninety-four skill areas. Winners from the national competition represent the United States in international skills competitions.

John Huhn, a student at Paul M. Hodgson Vocational Technical High School in Newark, Delaware, won the National SkillsUSA Championship in refrigeration in 2011. He was a member of Team USA at the World Skill competition in London, England, in October 2011. He credits his success to his instructors, Charlie Hoard, and Ed Karschner and other HVAC journeymen at Modern Controls, a Delaware commercial and industrial HVAC company. Since completing his high school work, Huhn has become an HVAC apprentice and continues to work at Modern Controls.

woodworking, among others. The increasing need for trained technicians in many industries has led to the development of high school curricula that emphasize technical courses.

One educational system that is emphasizing technology is in Ohio. Educators in central Ohio believe that "the 21st

Students at a Pennsylvania high school for automotive and mechanical engineering jump-start their careers while still in high school. Similar technical high schools are available for students interested in HVAC careers.

Century will reward workers who possess state-of-the-art technical and advanced academic skills." They established two technical centers to give students a head start in meeting the challenges of new technologies, including those important in the HVAC industry. Junior and senior students from high

schools in the sixteen participating central Ohio school districts can enroll in one of forty technical programs at these centers. Students are transported by bus to the career centers, where they receive their technical training. Academic studies are pursued at their home high schools. Students not only receive the academic credits they need for high school graduation, but they also earn college credits from Hocking College, one of Ohio's technical colleges located in Nelsonville. The Lancaster branch of Ohio University also participates in this program. No tuition is charged for these programs as long as the student resides in one of the participating school districts. The college credits earned are also free.

Students in the HVAC program learn skills in heating, cooling, ventilation, refrigeration, and customer service while working toward the EPA's universal certification that allows them to handle refrigerants.

Many other states have technical high schools with programs similar to the Ohio program. Students who successfully complete technical programs in high school are in great demand in vocational-technical colleges, community colleges, and university programs. Perhaps the greatest advantage of taking technical courses in high school, including HVAC courses, is finding out if a particular field of study is the right one to pursue for a lifetime career. If not, precious time and money need not be spent in college doing something that is unfulfilling. On the other hand, knowing that one has found a good career fit while in high school gives a person a step up in making decisions about further education.

chapter 3

EDUCATION OPTIONS FOR CAREERS IN HVAC

Training for jobs in the HVAC industry can be obtained in many ways: distance learning courses, vocational-technical schools, community colleges, and four-year colleges and universities. These options make a career in HVAC available to almost everyone.

DISTANCE LEARNING

Distance learning has had many definitions over the years. Initially, it was applied to correspondence courses in which instructors would supply students with reading lists, lessons, and examinations by mail. Today, it involves real-time television classes as well as online courses.

The common feature of distance learning programs is that teachers and students are not present in the same space. In other words, there are no defined classrooms. Students are freed from the necessity of traveling to a fixed place, at a fixed time, to meet a teacher and take a class.

Most distance learning courses now require that students have access to computers and know how to use them efficiently and effectively. They must also be able to work independently. A *lot* of self-discipline is needed for students to be successful in distance learning programs.

Many colleges and technical schools offer distance learning programs in HVAC. Most contract with ed2go, the largest provider of distance learning programs in the United States. More than two thousand colleges, universities, community-based organizations, unions, and the military use ed2go programs. The HVAC program provided by ed2go was developed by HVACRedu.net, a professional organization of HVACR educators working together to provide educational programs for

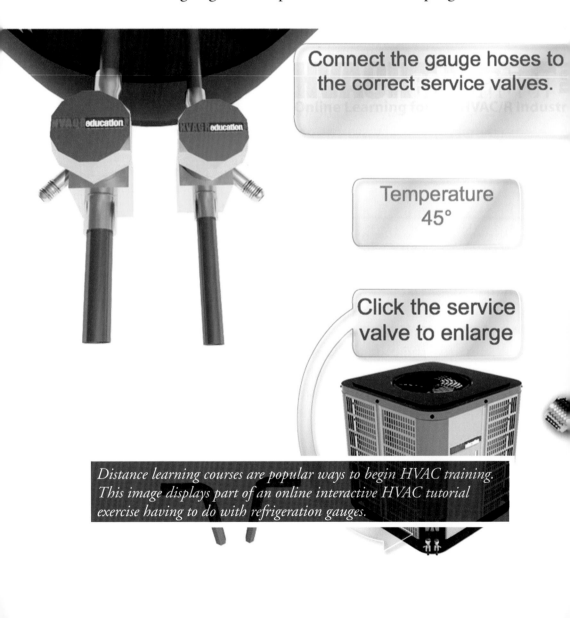

Distance learning courses are popular ways to begin HVAC training. This image displays part of an online interactive HVAC tutorial exercise having to do with refrigeration gauges.

the HVAC industry. This program has sixteen sections, each of which has six modules. Contained within the modules are reading assignments, Web site references, exercises, quizzes, video clips, animated images, and printable handouts covering specific HVAC concepts. Students have sixty days to complete each section of the course.

The program provides the book learning a student needs to apply for entry-level HVAC jobs, but not the hands-on experience he or she needs. Students must contact local contractors or HVAC technicians with whom they work to gain practical experience. At the end of each section of the course, the student must demonstrate to the supervising technician that he or she is competent in the subjects covered in that particular section.

VOCATIONAL-TECHNICAL SCHOOLS (VO-TECHS)

Vo-techs are schools in which students are taught the skills necessary to perform a specific job. Some cover several vocations, while others concentrate on a single vocation. The HVAC Technical Institute in Chicago, Illinois, specializes in HVAC. According to its brochure, the institute was established with one goal in mind: "to train men and women in practical skills

These students at the HVAC Technical Institute in Chicago, Illinois, are learning how to repair hydronic heating systems.

and knowledge in order to increase their worth in the heating, ventilation and air conditioning workplace."

The institute's course of study includes six modules: electricity, heating, basic air-conditioning, advanced air-conditioning, ventilation and installation, and hydronics (hot water and steam systems). The emphasis in these courses is on hands-on experience, although students also have regular lectures. To receive a graduation certificate, students must pass each module with a score of 70 percent or higher.

If considering a vo-tech, students should make sure the school is accredited by HVAC Excellence, the National Center for Construction Education and Research, or the Partnership for Air-Conditioning, Heating and Refrigeration Accreditation.

COMMUNITY COLLEGES

Community colleges also provide technical training in HVAC. Unlike vocational schools, however, community colleges require students to take at least a few general education courses. One of the major attractions of community colleges is that students can usually choose between certificate programs that can be completed in only a few months or

CHECK IT OUT!

American School Search (ASS) is a comprehensive online resource designed specifically for future college students and their parents. It lists 6,670 colleges throughout the United States and provides honest, accurate, and up-to-date information for each school. Even more helpful, the site lists colleges by program of study and by state. Of the 6,670 colleges reviewed by the ASS, 712 offer programs in HVAC. Six hundred seventy of the colleges offer certificate programs, 227 offer associate's degree programs, and four offer bachelor's degrees in HVAC.

According to the ASS, becoming an HVAC technician is a very popular choice for students today because of the short amount of time it takes for them to start earning a salary. The ASS also points out that the top HVAC schools usually guarantee almost immediate job placement for their trainees.

By visiting this Web site, students can get a broad overview of HVAC programs, the good and bad points of various programs, and the relative cost of each. It is a great place to start, so check it out at http://www.american-school-search.com.

courses that lead to an associate's degree. Associate's degree programs usually take two years to complete.

Manchester Community College, in Manchester, New Hampshire, is one of many community colleges that offer associate's degrees in HVAC technology. An abbreviated schedule for the two-year program is as follows:

YEAR ONE			
Fall Semester		**Spring Semester**	
Course	Credits	Course	Credits
Fundamentals of Refrigeration I	4	Fundamentals of Refrigeration II	4
Related Electricity I	4	Related Electricity II	4
Fundamentals of Heating I	4	Fundamentals of Heating II	4
College Composition	4	Numerical Algebra and Trigonometry	3
Numerical Geometry	3	Social Science Elective	3
College Success Seminar	3		

YEAR TWO			
Fall Semester		**Spring Semester**	
Course	Credits	Course	Credits
Commercial Refrigeration	4	Air-Conditioning and Heat Pumps	5
Hydronics and Steam Systems	4	Warm Air Systems	5
Introductory Physics	3	Foreign language, Humanities or Fine Arts Elective	3
Microsoft Computer Application	3	English Elective	3

FOUR-YEAR COLLEGES

Four-year colleges may also offer certificate and associate's programs in HVAC. Most HVAC students who attend four-year colleges, however, are interested in obtaining a bachelor's degree in HVAC design or engineering. HVAC engineering is usually a specialty area of study within the mechanical engineering curriculum. Broad academic coursework, in addition to core

This student at Grand Rapids Community College in Michigan practices climbing skills that he will need so that he can work safely in the new, green energy world of wind turbines.

HVAC subjects, is required for HVAC engineering bachelor's degrees.

Lewis-Clark State College in Lewiston, Idaho, has an acclaimed HVAC program. It offers three levels of study in HVAC. A certification program offers three different certificates depending on the student's main area of interest. An associate's degree program incorporates the HVAC courses needed to earn a certificate with general education courses. The college also offers a bachelor's degree in HVAC. This degree builds on the associate's degree, requiring additional general education courses.

SCHOLARSHIPS

Getting an education can be expensive. Fortunately, there are scholarships available to assist qualified students in paying their tuition and other expenses. Several Internet sites offer free scholarship searches, and others give information about specific scholarships. CollegeScholarships.org lists community sources of scholarships for those wanting careers in the HVAC industry. It also lists HVAC associations and individual colleges that offer scholarships for HVAC students.

HVAC students in Maine, for instance, should contact the Maine

Community Foundation for information about the Leland R. Dahlgren Scholarship Fund. This fund provides financial assistance to students seeking two- or four-year degrees in construction careers such as HVAC.

An example of an HVAC organization that offers scholarships is the Air-Conditioning, Heating, and Refrigeration Institute (AHRI). This organization established the Clifford H. "Ted" Rees Jr. Scholarship Foundation "to assist with recruitment and competency of future HVACR technicians." The foundation awards as many as fifteen scholarships each

Joseph J. Morrill works in an engineering technology lab at the University of Southern Maine. While attending Yarmouth High School, Morrill received the 2012 Leland Dahlgren Scholarship, which helped him to become an engineering technology and chemistry major at the university.

year. Each pays up to $2,000 to a student enrolled in an accred-ited HVAC program.

The American Society of Heating, Refrigerating and Air-Conditioning Engineers also provides scholarships. Many other HVAC organizations, as well as several unions in the construc-tion industry, offer HVAC scholarships. Most of these are listed on the Web sites of the organizations.

Two colleges that offer scholarships specifically to HVAC students are Dunwoody College of Technology in Minneapolis, Minnesota, and Joliet Junior College in Joliet, Illinois. Both offer at least three scholarships each year to HVAC students. When students investigate HVAC programs, they should inquire about the availability of scholarships.

chapter 4

EARN WHILE YOU LEARN

To train for a career and get paid while doing it is a win-win situation! People who get their HVAC training while serving in one of the branches of the U.S. or Canadian militaries and HVAC technicians who train through the U.S. Job Corps are among those lucky enough to earn while they learn. The same is true for those who serve HVAC apprenticeships during the course of their training.

HVAC TRAINING IN THE MILITARY

During the enlistment process, recruits for all branches of the U.S. military take a series of tests called the Armed Forces Vocational Aptitude Battery. Scores from these tests, along with other information about recruits, help determine which jobs the recruits will be trained for and what they will do during their military careers.

Soldiers trained as HVAC technicians are classified as utilities equipment repairers. They receive four weeks and three days of training at Aberdeen Proving Grounds in Maryland before beginning their military HVAC careers. Marine HVAC technicians are called refrigeration and air conditioning technicians. Marines also train at Aberdeen Proving Grounds.

A senior airman who is an HVAC technician services air-conditioning equipment in the control tower at Ellsworth Air Force Base, South Dakota.

HVAC technicians in the navy are called refrigeration and air conditioning systems technicians. In the air force, those who do HVAC work are called HVAC technicians or specialists. They get HVAC training in the Electrical Technology School at Sheppard Air Force Base in Texas.

Members of the military receive their training while earning military wages appropriate to their ranks. These salaries change from year to year and are listed on several Web sites. In addition to their base salaries, all military personnel receive a variety of allowances, such as housing and food allowances. They also receive basic medical care and biweekly living allowances, all of which are welcome additions to their base salaries.

Canadian military forces have refrigeration and mechanical systems technicians (RM tech). The RM tech job is one of seven construction engineering occupations supporting Canadian forces worldwide. Following thirteen weeks of basic training, those being trained as RM techs are sent to the Canadian Forces School of Military Engineering in Gagetown, New Brunswick. They spend twenty-four weeks learning basic HVAC skills before being sent to one of four units: the Construction Engineering Flight (air force), Construction Troop (army), Naval Construction Troop (navy), or the Base/Wing/Formation Construction Engineering Section.

HVAC TRAINING IN THE U.S. JOB CORPS

The U.S. Job Corps, established in 1964 by the U.S. Department of Labor, is the nation's largest career technical training and education program. It is available to students from low-income families who are between the ages of sixteen and twenty-four. More than 100,000 students each year receive hands-on training in one of 100 technical training programs at 125 centers across the United States at no expense to themselves. In addition to job training, a Job Corps participant receives free housing and food, basic medical care, and a small living allowance.

The Job Corps' HVAC training program takes eight to twelve months to complete. It is a comprehensive program that covers not only technical skills but also skills to enhance a student's ability to meet, communicate, and work with customers. In addition, HVAC students are trained in a variety of green subjects to prepare for successful careers in the new green economy. Students who complete the program are eligible to receive one or more certifications through the National Center for Construction Education and Research (NCCER).

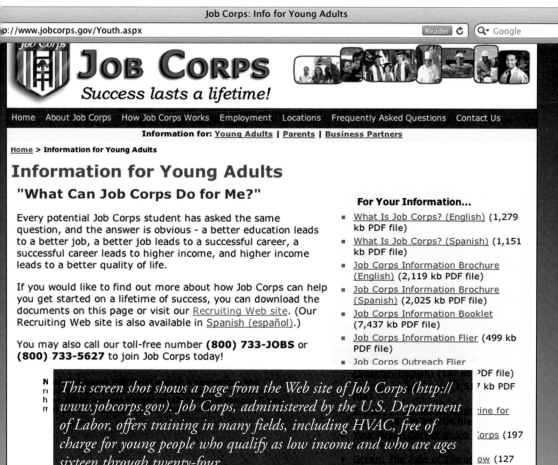

This screen shot shows a page from the Web site of Job Corps (http://www.jobcorps.gov). Job Corps, administered by the U.S. Department of Labor, offers training in many fields, including HVAC, free of charge for young people who qualify as low income and who are ages sixteen through twenty-four.

NEWEST JOB CORPS CENTER FEATURES HVAC TECHNOLOGY

The 125th Job Corps Center opened its doors in January 2011 in Milwaukee, Wisconsin. The center not only provides classrooms and laboratories, but also dormitories, a health care center, a cafeteria, and several recreational facilities for as many as three hundred students. HVAC is one of the training programs featured at the center. In an article by Georgia Pabst, a reporter for the *Milwaukee Journal Sentinel*, the center's director, Jim Roberts, said, "Job Corps is not a handout, but a hand-up program to give the next level of opportunity so that young people can support themselves and become taxpaying citizens."

One of the first students to enter the center's HVAC program was featured in Pabst's article. Lavarre Buchanan is a Milwaukee native who struggled to finish high school while working in a packing and shipping company. After finding out he was to be a father, he realized he needed to make some changes in his life. In his interview with Pabst he said, "I made up my mind that I had to better myself and I started looking at different programs." The opening of the new Job Corps center coincided with his search. The Job Corps was a "good fit" for him. He chose to participate in the HVAC training program while completing work for his high school diploma.

HVAC APPRENTICESHIPS

HVAC apprenticeships are programs that allow a student to combine classroom work with on-the-job training (OJT). While students pay tuition for the classroom portion of their training, they receive regular salaries for OJT. At the end of the apprenticeship, they are qualified as journey-level HVAC technicians. In states that require licensure, they are also qualified to take licensure examinations.

There are several HVAC apprenticeship programs throughout the United States and Canada. In choosing an apprenticeship program, students should be certain that the program falls under the National Apprenticeship Act. The U.S. Department of Labor works with state agencies to oversee and manage all apprenticeship programs within a state that fall under this act. State apprenticeship agencies work with HVAC industry organizations, labor unions, individual companies, and educational institutions to establish and oversee their programs.

An example of an HVAC apprenticeship is the one offered by the Plumbing, Heating, and Cooling Contractors of Iowa (PHCC). The apprenticeship is certified by the U.S. Department of Labor. The program requires 144 hours of classroom work and 2,000 hours of OJT. Students get OJT as employees of local HVAC companies. They are supervised by HVAC journeymen/women. Upon successful completion of the apprenticeship, students become certified journey-level workers. They also meet the requirements for licensure in Iowa. In 2010, Iowa passed a law requiring all new HVAC technicians to complete a four-year approved apprenticeship and pass a state licensure exam in order to be licensed in the state.

In general, the salary of beginning HVAC apprentices is about half of what journey-level technicians earn. As they complete classroom work and gain additional hours of OJT, their salaries increase until they are receiving a journey-level wage at the time of completion of their training.

To find out about approved apprenticeship opportunities, students should contact the apprenticeship and training division of their state governments or go to Web sites of the various HVAC organizations and unions for information.

Students seeking apprenticeships in Canada can get information from the governments of individual Canadian provinces. An example of a very useful publication for those seeking apprenticeships in Ontario is the *Apprenticeship Subject Pathways*.

Most apprenticeship programs provide HVAC students with hands-on training in testing HVAC equipment and other job skills.

This publication is available on the Web site of the Ministry of Education and the Ministry of Training, Colleges, and Universities of Ontario

Canadian HVAC apprentices must complete nine thousand hours (about four-and-a-half years) of training. Three levels of theoretical (classroom) training are required. The remaining hours of training are obtained while working with qualified HVAC technicians. As in the United States, beginning apprentices earn about half of what a journeyman HVAC technician makes. Salaries are increased as more training is completed.

chapter 5

CERTIFICATIONS AND LICENSES

With the exception of people who have taken formal HVAC apprenticeships, most students who complete their HVAC training have inadequate amounts of practical experience to qualify as fully trained, journey-level HVAC technicians. They enter the workforce in entry-level jobs where they work under the supervision of fully trained technicians until they have at least two thousand hours of practical experience. This period usually takes about two years. They are then qualified to take the examinations to become journeymen/women. Once that credential is obtained, they can apply for a license to practice in the state or states in which they want to work.

EMPLOYMENT READY CERTIFICATION

Students who have completed HVAC courses of study are eager to go to work. Before they can do that, however, they must show that they have mastered the basic knowledge and skills needed for entry-level jobs. Attaining industry-recognized certifications is one way a student can document his or her competence. These certifications are the rewards for passing certification examinations. The three organizations most commonly involved in the certification process are HVAC

Excellence, North American Technician Excellence (NATE), and the Environmental Protection Agency (EPA).

HVAC Excellence is a nonprofit organization that was founded in 1994. It has two main goals. The first goal is to set the standards that HVAC training programs must meet. It also monitors programs to make sure they adhere to the standards. The second is to administer examinations to students in HVAC training programs to demonstrate their competency in the subjects they are studying. Students who successfully complete

This is the home page for HVAC Excellence (http://www.hvacexcellence.org), which is an organization that sets the standards for HVAC training programs. The organization also administers examinations to HVAC students to test their competency in HVAC subjects.

HVAC Excellence approved training programs receive Employment Ready Certifications showing that they have the knowledge and skill to work in entry-level jobs.

Most students also qualify for at least one certification from the EPA while in training programs. Section 608 of the Federal Clean Air Act requires that anyone working with regulated refrigerants, or disposing of appliances with refrigerants, have at least one of four EPA certifications. To obtain any section 608 certification, the applicant must pass an examination with twenty-five core knowledge questions, plus twenty-five questions in the area of the certification.

Another organization that is extremely important in HVAC certification processes is North American Technician Excellence. NATE is the only third-party, independent certifying body for HVAC professionals. It provides no study materials or training programs. Its only goal is to provide examinations that, if successfully completed, highlight a technician's competency in specific skills within the industry. Since it is totally independent, certification by NATE is highly regarded. NATE offers multiple certifications for both HVAC installers and HVAC service technicians.

There are no specific educational requirements or work experience needed to take NATE certification examinations. Those who feel they can pass the exams can take them. NATE strongly suggests, however, that candidates have at least one year of training, including some work experience, to take the examination for certification as an HVAC installation technician and two years of training to take the HVAC service technician examination. A person who passes the examination for service technician certification automatically receives certification as an installation technician.

The examination for service technician certification includes a core test that has fifty questions on safety, tool usage, electrical maintenance, heat transfer principles, and basic construction.

A service technician monitors equipment that is undergoing extreme environmental testing. There are no particular educational prerequisites or prior work experience involved in taking NATE certification examinations. NATE recommends, though, that candidates have at least two years of training and some work experience before taking the exam for HVAC service technician.

EMPLOYERS WANT NATE CERTIFIED TECHNICIANS!

Although NATE knew that the technicians it certified were in high demand by employers, the reasons for this demand had not been studied. In 2006, NATE asked Matt Michel of Service Roundtable to devise a study to see if technicians with NATE certification were indeed more valuable to a company than noncertified technicians. The study was called the "NATE Impact Study." Service Roundtable is an organization that was founded by a group of leading contractors to share information and help other contractors improve sales, marketing, operations, and profitability. The study, an online survey, was distributed to companies who employed at least one NATE-certified technician and one noncertified technician. A total of forty pairs of technicians were evaluated. After analyzing the data from the survey, it was found that each NATE-certified technician increased a company's profitability by about $10,000 each year. Noncertified technicians did not. NATE-certified technicians had more experience than noncertified technicians, so they made fewer mistakes and generated fewer callbacks. They also helped their employers retain customers because the competence of NATE-certified technicians was obvious to the customers with whom they worked. What employer wouldn't prefer to employ NATE-certified technicians?

A passing grade of 70 percent must be made on this test. After completing the core test, the candidate takes a one-hunded-question test in one of ten specialty areas. These areas include air-conditioning, air distribution, air-to-air heat pumps, gas furnaces, oil furnaces, hydronics-gas, hydronics-oil, light commercial refrigeration, and commercial refrigeration. The examination is meant to test the candidate's knowledge of the installation and maintenance of these HVAC/R systems. The core test and the specialty test must be completed within four hours. Having NATE certification moves a technician to the head of the line of those seeking HVAC entry-level jobs.

ENTRY-LEVEL TECHNICIAN TO JOURNEY-LEVEL TECHNICIAN

Newly graduated technicians with Employment Ready Certifications from HVAC Excellence or entry-level certifications from NATE, who have not completed apprenticeship programs, are now ready to get the two thousand hours of OJT they need to become journey-level technicians. IntelliTec College, in Colorado Springs, Colorado, has a highly respected HVAC training program. In an article written by Shivaun Martynes, IntelliTec's HVAC program director, Eric Seltenright, gives advice on how to find and get hired for entry-level HVAC jobs. He suggests either applying for a union-sponsored apprentice program that will provide the OJT needed or seeking employment in one of three places: large HVAC equipment manufacturing companies like Trane, Honeywell, or Hobart; commercial or residential HVAC service companies; or in facility HVAC departments. These facilities might include hotels, schools, hospitals, colleges, large sport venues, and government offices that require around-the-clock, on-site maintenance personnel. He believes the top three things that employers look for in candidates applying for HVAC jobs are the three A's: appearance; attitude; and aptitude. He said, "Remember, employers could be more interested in your attendance and dependability than your grades."

Once the required OJT is obtained, a person can apply to take examinations for journey-level certification. This exam is an open-book test that covers HVAC topics as well as codes that must be met within the industry.

After completing coursework at the HVAC Technical Institute in Chicago, students must still complete two thousand hours of on-the-job training before being eligible for journey-level certification. These students are working on refrigeration exercises.

LICENSURE

After obtaining their journey-level certifications, technicians can apply for licensure within the states where they want to work. Licensure requirements vary widely from state to state. Iowa, for example requires that new HVAC technicians complete a four-year approved apprenticeship before applying to take the state licensure examination. California, on the other hand, has no specific educational requirements. However, a person must have four years of non-trainee OJT. In other words, an applicant must work as a journeyman for four years for a contractor or an HVAC company before he or she can apply for licensure. He or she must then pass two state examinations: the California HVAC Trade Exam and the California Law and Business Exam for Contractors. Information about what is required for licensure in particular states can be obtained from the state licensure boards of each state. A Web site that is especially useful for looking at licensure requirements is http://www.nationalcontractors.com/licensing. This site lists the requirements for licensure in each state including the address and phone number of licensing boards. It also provides other information unique to each state's licensing procedure.

chapter 6

ON THE JOB!

T he BLS reports that in 2010 there were 267,800 HVAC technicians in the workforce. Drafters, design engineers, and HVAC engineers increase the number of people working in the industry, but there is still a shortage of people to fill all the jobs. Those who do choose jobs in the industry find that salaries, compensation packages, and other benefits are among the highest and best in the construction trades.

SALARY

Salaries for HVAC professionals reflect the level of education and amount of work experience that each person has. Those in entry-level jobs, as well as those in apprenticeship programs, earn approximately half of the salary of journey-level technicians. Information on current salaries can be obtained from the BLS Web site (http://www.bls.gov) or by reviewing Web sites such as PayScale.com.

A basic education in HVAC can usually be completed within two years. Therefore, HVAC technicians can begin entry-level jobs long before four-year college graduates break into the workforce. A survey of salaries earned by four-year college graduates in 2011–2012 was published on PayScale.com. The average income of a journey-level HVAC technician exceeds salaries listed there for most teachers, nurses, social workers, ministers, chefs, and those graduating with fine arts degrees. With the apprenticeships and scholarships that are available in the industry, many HVAC technicians start to work with little school debt that must be repaid. Consequently, over their working lifetimes, HVAC technicians make more money than many people with four-year college degrees.

The BLS says that one in six HVAC technicians is a member of a union. A labor union is an organized group of workers who join together to better everyday working conditions for everyone. Through union membership, workers can influence wages, work hours, benefits, workplace health and safety, and other work-related issues. Some work places require all the workers hired to become union members and some don't. Union workers generally earn higher wages than their nonunion counterparts. This benefit may be counterbalanced by the need to pay union dues and by having fewer

One in six HVAC technicians is a member of a union. The Plumbers and Steamfitters Union is one to which HVAC technicians may belong. Here, Local 21 union members march in a parade.

job options. There are more nonunion HVAC jobs available than union jobs.

COMPENSATION PACKAGES

Many workers consider compensation packages, which may include medical insurance and retirement plans, as important as the salaries they receive. Compensation packages are usually specific to the company for which a technician works. When considering options for employment, people should decide what, other than salary, is important and choose the job that best meets their needs. The more certificates of excellence, like those offered by NATE, a person has, the more valuable he or she is to an employer. This advantage is often reflected in the compensation package offered to the employee.

OTHER GREAT ASPECTS OF HVAC JOBS

One of the most attractive aspects of HVAC as a profession is that HVAC technicians and other workers are needed almost everywhere. A career in HVAC is a mobile one. If a person starts working in an HVAC service company in his or her hometown and decides to explore a different part of the world, there is likely to be an HVAC job available. The profession also allows for many areas of specialization. For instance, a person who loves airplanes can specialize in aviation climate control. Those drawn to the sea can specialize in the maintenance and repair of climate control systems on ships or even find jobs working in the highly specialized field of marine aquariums. HVAC technicians can tailor their careers by choosing continuing education courses that give special certifications in the areas of their greatest interest. Because this is a dynamic industry, these educational opportunities will expand as new technologies develop.

WORKING CONDITIONS

Working conditions within the HVAC industry vary with the job that a technician does. According to the BLS, 55 percent of technicians work for building contractors. Most of their work is indoors, although they may work on outdoor heat pumps, air-conditioning units, cooling towers, or other equipment. This work may need to be done even in bad weather. Technicians often work in awkward and cramped spaces that may be uncomfortable, especially if air conditioners or heating systems are broken.

Most technicians work full-time with occasional weekend and evening shifts. During peak heating and cooling seasons, they might work a lot of overtime.

Although HVAC jobs are not considered to be high risk, on-the-job injuries can happen. The most common injuries are

Rooftop industrial-sized HVAC systems like this one are common on large buildings such as Harrah's Resort and Casino in Lake Tahoe, Nevada. Working conditions for those in the HVAC industry change depending on the situation, and they can be hot, cold, high, low, indoors, or outdoors.

AN INTERVIEW WITH ALLEN SNYDER

Allen Snyder recently retired from a long career in the facilities engineering department of Harrah's Resort and Casino in Lake Tahoe, Nevada. Over the course of his years of employment, he saved the resort more than $5 million by modifying and improving the climate control systems of the facility. He was never bored with his job! He answered the following questions during an interview with the author:

Q: From what background did you come to work at Harrah's?

Mr. Snyder: I grew up on farms in Iowa, where it was necessary to fix things that broke rather than waiting for a repairman. By the time I went to college, there weren't many things I couldn't repair. The technical engineering courses I took filled in the gaps in my theoretical knowledge of how many types of machines, including computers, work. After that, it was a matter of applying what I had learned. I began working as a mechanic in the engineering department at Harrah's and advanced to a supervisory position. The second half of my career at Harrah's was as energy manager.

Q: What energy saving innovations did you bring to Harrah's?

Mr. Snyder: Although there were many others, there were two changes that were very significant in saving energy. The first was relatively simple. We covered the hotel's west-facing windows with a thin film that decreased the summer greenhouse effect in those rooms. This resulted in a considerable reduction in the amount of electricity needed for air-conditioning.

The second change involved installing variable frequency drives (VFD) in many of the fans in the building. During hot summer days and when casinos are busy, fans in the HVAC system need to run at maximum rates to provide adequate fresh conditioned air. In cooler and less busy times, that isn't necessary. With VFDs, we were able to control the rate at which fans ran. This saved a lot of electricity over the long haul.

From the standpoint of saving money, the most significant thing I did was to design and help construct a pipeline that carried natural gas directly from a feeder source to Harrah's and three other casinos in the area. By buying gas from the producer, rather than a middleman, the cost of the gas was much lower.

Q: Do you have any advice for young people considering careers as HVAC technicians or engineers?

Mr. Snyder: I would certainly say, "Go for it!" If you love machines and working with them, you have great opportunities ahead. I'm astounded at the advances that have been made in energy management during my working career. Those are minimal compared with what must and will occur in the future. Our planet needs your help. Lucky you!

muscle strains caused by lifting heavy loads. Because most HVAC work is done overhead, shoulder and neck strains may also occur. Hand injuries including scrapes and burns are commonplace.

WOMEN IN THE HVAC INDUSTRY

HVAC remains a nontraditional profession for women. According to a report prepared by the U.S. Congress Joint Economic Committee entitled "Women and the Economy

Only 0.7 percent of HVAC professionals are women. More women are entering the field each year, drawn by good salaries and the stability of the industry.

2010: 25 Years of Progress but Challenges Remain," women make up 50 percent of those working in the United States. Fifty percent of all women in the United States have jobs outside the home. In spite of this large number of women in the workforce, only 0.7 percent of HVAC professionals are women.

Many leaders in the HVAC industry are working on strategies to make the industry more attractive to women. It is likely that efforts being made now to present the HVAC industry to middle and high school students will prompt more young women to pursue HVAC as a profession.

chapter 7

HVAC Is "Going Green"

The term "going green" means different things to different people. For the HVAC industry, it means finding ways to conserve energy and benefit the environment by reducing waste and pollution. While HVAC designers and engineers build new types of HVAC equipment that conserve energy, eliminate harmful emissions, and improve air quality, HVAC technicians are learning to install, maintain, and repair them. Green HVAC systems are the future of the industry.

TECHNOLOGIES FOR A GREEN HVAC INDUSTRY

Technological advancements in HVAC equipment are being made on a daily basis. In some cases, these advancements involve making changes in existing pieces of equipment to make them more efficient. In other cases, it means taking old ideas, adding new twists, and coming up with completely new products. The following innovative, new HVAC technologies are only a few examples of how HVAC is going green.

MAGNETIC REFRIGERATION SYSTEMS

In 1880, German physicist Emil Warburg (1846–1931) observed a phenomenon called the magnetocaloric effect. He noted that certain metallic materials, when placed in a magnetic field, changed temperatures. The first refrigeration system that used the magnetocaloric effect was produced in 1933. The system was very expensive to produce, so it never became commercially available.

That is about to change! A magnetic refrigerator has been developed by the Whirlpool Corporation, in partnership with Camfridge, a U.K. refrigeration company. Refrigeration systems based on the same principles will hopefully be available for use in green homes and businesses in the near future.

Instead of using compressors, magnetic refrigeration systems use shallow containers of metallic materials as refrigerants. As the containers are moved into a magnetic field, the refrigerants get hot. Heat produced in the process is transferred to a heat transfer fluid, usually a water mixture, and is removed from the system. As the heat is transferred, the refrigerants cool down. When the magnetic field is removed, the refrigerants become even colder. The degree of cooling that occurs depends on the type of refrigerant used. Heat from food in the refrigerator can then be transferred to the cooled refrigerants in the containers. As a result, the inside of the refrigerator and its contents are kept cool. Karl Gschneidner, a senior metallurgist at the U.S. Department of Energy's Ames Laboratory in Iowa, says that magnetic cooling and refrigeration may be as much as 30 percent more energy efficient than conventional vapor compression refrigeration. Because the refrigerants are solid, they can't escape into the atmosphere and deplete the ozone layer. This makes magnetic refrigeration very environmentally clean. HVACR technicians are now being credentialed to work with magnetic air-conditioning and other magnetic refrigeration systems.

WASTE HEAT RECOVERY SYSTEMS

Almost all industries in the United State use machines that produce heat. Most of this heat, which is a form of energy, is wasted. Imagine the amount of energy that could be saved if waste heat could be harnessed to do work! That is exactly what green HVAC systems are doing.

Nowhere is waste heat more valued than in Antarctica. Carol Fey, an author and HVAC technical trainer, spent four months working at McMurdo Station in Antarctica with Mike Blachut, a veteran HVAC technician who has worked there for fifteen years. In an article that she wrote after returning from

Waste heat is an energy source at the Research Station at McMurdo Sound, Antarctica. Waste heat from the power plant helps desalination of the seawater in the station's water production plant.

the station, she discussed the value of waste heat to the facility. She says that for every 1,700 kilowatts (kW) of energy produced at McMurdo Station's power plant, about one-third goes up the exhaust stack as waste heat. Another one-third is given off as waste heat by radiators located on the generators in the power plant. The remaining one-third of the energy is converted to electricity. Initially, only waste heat from the radiators could be recovered. It was used to power a hydronic heating

WILL COMPUTERS HEAT HOMES?

Rebecca Rosen, an associate editor of the *Atlantic* magazine, has written an article discussing a research report from computer giant Microsoft. She says that the computer industry consumes 2 percent of America's total energy each year. Most of it is used to cool data centers and the computer servers they contain. She also points out that home heating systems use about 6 percent of America's energy during cooler months of the year. Microsoft has proposed the development of a device called a data furnace that would allow both the computer industry and homeowners to reduce their energy costs.

Microsoft describes a data furnace as "a mini cloud server" that contains forty to four hundred computer central processing units (CPU). The server would be hooked directly into a home's HVAC system. The waste heat given off by the CPUs would be used to warm homes during colder months of the year. When homes do not need to be heated, the waste heat would be used for clothes drying or water heating. While this idea has merit, there are many bugs that must be worked out of the system before it becomes functional. "Nevertheless," Rosen says, "the basic idea that we can combine two inefficiencies in a way that reduces overall energy consumption is the kind of thinking necessary for making America more efficient over the long haul."

system using equal parts of water and glycol, a type of alcohol. The heated water mixture was circulated to nine of the station's buildings and kept them warm even when outdoor temperatures were well below 0° F (-18° C). Recently, the development of direct digital computer controls has made it possible to recover part of the waste heat from the power plant's exhaust stack to add to the radiator heat.

Waste heat is also used in the station's water production plant. It is necessary to remove salt from seawater to make the 55,000 gallons (208,198 liters) of fresh water needed at the station each day. Seawater has a temperature of 26 to 28°F (-3.3 to −2.2°C) in Antarctica. Before it can be desalinated, it must be warmed to 40° F (4.4°C). Waste heat is used for the warming process.

GEOTHERMAL TECHNOLOGIES

Geothermal technologies are those that harness heat from within the earth for some use. One of the newest of these technologies involves drilling wells into large underground reservoirs of hot water. These reservoirs can be found throughout the western United States and in many other countries, such as Iceland and New Zealand. Steam and hot water from wells are pumped into power plants to provide energy to generate electricity. Hot water can also be piped directly into hydronic heating systems in homes and businesses. The advantage of using steam and hot water as the fuel for generating electricity is that they are renewable resources. The process is very clean; it doesn't produce smoke or greenhouse gases that damage the atmosphere.

Another application of geothermal technology is the development of geothermal heat pumps. These heat pumps are also called ground source heat pumps. An article on geothermal heat pumps from the U.S. Department of Energy says that these heat pumps work because, beneath its surface, the earth remains at a relatively constant temperature throughout the year. It is warmer than the air aboveground during the winter

An HVAC technician inspects a geothermal HVAC system. Geothermal heat pumps transfer heat from the earth into buildings in the winter and draw heat out of buildings in summer.

and cooler in the summer. A geothermal heat pump transfers heat stored in the earth into a building during winter and draws heat out of buildings in summer months.

HVAC technicians with an interest in geothermal technologies can become geothermal heat pump engineers or geothermal HVAC engineers. Several HVAC organizations offer courses of study and certifications in this new green technology.

These are just a few examples of how the HVAC industry is going green. New HVAC professionals will have almost unlimited opportunities to support the goals of the green movement—conserving energy, protecting the environment, and making the world a safer and healthier place to live.

glossary

academic Describing education that is general or liberal, rather than technical or vocational.

accredited When an institution of learning is recognized as maintaining the required standards for its graduates to gain admission to other reputable institutions of higher learning; having achieved credentials for professional practice.

blueprint A photographic reproduction in white on a blue background of architectural or engineering plans.

coalition An association of groups of people who join together for a particular cause.

component One of the many parts of a structure or system.

curriculum A special course of study or, collectively, all the courses of study in a school.

diagnose To identify the source of a problem within a system.

ductwork The pipes or tubes through which air from air conditioners, furnaces, or ventilation systems is carried throughout a building.

efficient Producing the desired result with the least effort, expense, or waste.

Environmental Protection Agency (EPA) A U.S. government agency created in 1970 for the purpose of protecting the environment and human health.

forum An opportunity for people to discuss individual viewpoints on a particular topic.

greenhouse effect The warming of Earth and its lower atmosphere, caused by trapped solar radiation. The term is also used to describe the heat generated in a room by sunlight passing through windows.

heat pump A device for cooling an enclosed space by pumping hot air out and for warming it by extracting heat from outdoor air, subsurface soil, or from a hot-water source and pumping it into the space.

hydronics The science of heating by the forced circulation of a hot liquid or gas (hot water and steam).

magnetic field The space around a magnet in which the magnet's power is very strong.

malfunction To fail to work correctly or properly.

mechanical engineering A profession related to the study and use of machines that transform, transmit, or use energy, force, and motion for a specific purpose.

module A unit of something that has a specific purpose; for instance, a unit of study on a particular topic.

refrigerant A substance used to cool off an enclosed space. This could be ice, several different types of gas, or even metals that change temperature in magnetic fields.

thermostat A device for regulating temperature, especially one that automatically controls a furnace or air conditioner.

tuition The money paid for a specific course of instruction or class.

for more information

Air Conditioning Contractors of America (ACCA)
2800 Shirlington Road, Suite 300
Arlington, VA 22206
(703) 575-4477
Web site: http://www.acca.org
The ACCA is an organization that helps HVAC contractors
    acquire, serve, and satisfy customers. It offers various
    training programs for HVAC technicians.

Air-Conditioning, Heating, and Refrigeration Institute (AHRI)
2111 Wilson Boulevard, Suite 500
Arlington, VA 22201
(703) 600-0377
Web site: http://www.ahri.net
This trade association represents manufacturers of more
    than 90 percent of all HVAC equipment in the United
    States. It provides training programs and competency
    examinations.

American Society of Heating, Refrigeration and Air-
    Conditioning Engineers (ASHRAE)
1791 Tullie Circle NE
Atlanta, GA 30329
(404) 636-8400
Web site: http://www.ashrae.org
ASHRAE is a building technology society that does many
    things, including providing training programs and
    scholarships for future HVAC engineers.

Heating, Refrigeration and Air Conditioning Institute of
  Canada (HRAI)
5045 Orbitor Drive, Building 11, Suite 300
Mississauga, ON L4W 4Y4
Canada
(800) 267-2231
Web site: http://www.hrai.ca
The HRAI represents HVAC manufacturers, wholesalers, and
  contractors in Canada.

HVAC Excellence
1701 Pennsylvania Avenue NW
Washington, DC 20006
(800) 394-5268
Web site: http://www.hvacexcellence.org
HVAC Excellence is a nonprofit organization founded in
  1994 to improve technical competence in the HVAC
  industry.

Job Corps
200 Constitution Avenue NW, Suite N4463
Washington, DC 20210
(202) 693-3000
Web site: http://www.jobcorps.gov
The Job Corps, a progam administered by the U.S.
  Department of Labor, provides career technical training
  and education for students between the ages of sixteen and
  twenty-four.

Ministry of Training, Colleges, and Universities
Mowat Block, Fourteenth Floor
900 Bay Street
Toronto, ON M7A 1L2

Canada
(416) 325-2929
Web site: http://www.tcu.gov.on.ca
The ministry has information about applying for HVAC
apprenticeships in Canada

North American Technician Excellence (NATE)
4100 North Fairfax Drive, Suite 210
Arlington, VA 22203
(703) 276-7247
Web site: http://www.natex.org
NATE is an independent agency providing certification
examinations for the HVAC industry.

Plumbing-Heating-Cooling Contractors Association (PHCC)
180 South Washington Street
Falls Church, VA 22046
(703) 237-8100
Web site: http://www.naphcc.org
PHCC is the oldest trade association in the construction
industry. It had the industry's first apprenticeship program.

Refrigeration Service Engineers Society of Canada (RSES)
P.O. Box 3, Station B
Etobicoke, ON M9W 5K9
Canada
(877) 955-6255
Web site: http://www.rsescanada.com
The RSES of Canada conducts educational meetings, technical
credentialing programs, and training courses for the Canadian
HVAC industry.

U.S. Bureau of Labor Statistics (BLS)
Division of Information and Marketing Services

2 Massachusetts Avenue NE, Room 2850
Washington, DC 20212
(202) 691-5200
Web site: http://www.bls.gov
The BLS provides career guides to and statistics on careers in
   various industries, includig HVAC.

U.S. Green Building Council
2101 L Street NW, Suite 500
Washington, DC 20037
(800) 795-1747
Web site: http://www.usgbc.org
USGBC is made up of tens of thousands of member organizations that are dedicated to improving energy efficiency in
   the building trades.

Women in HVACR
P.O. Box 2206
Orland Park, IL 60462
(708) 417-5946
Web site: http://www.womeninhvacr.org
This is the premier organization for women in the HVAC
   industry. It provides multiple avenues to women to con-
   nect and grow both professionally and personally.

WEB SITES

Due to the changing nature of Internet links, Rosen
Publishing has developed an online list of Web sites related to
the subject of this book. This site is updated regularly. Please
use this link to access the list:

http://www.rosenlinks.com/ECAR/HVAC

for further reading

Brain, Marshall. *How Stuff Works*. Edison, NY: Chartwell Books, 2010.

Carson, Rachel. *Silent Spring*. New York, NY: Mariner Books, 2007.

Christen, Carol, and Richard Bolles. *What Color Is Your Parachute? For Teens Discovering Yourself, Defining Your Future*. Rev. ed. Berkley, CA: Ten Speed Press, 2010.

Cox, Stanley. *Losing Our Cool*. New York, NY: The New Press, 2010.

Gischman, C. *Last Pick on the Planet*. Lincoln, NE: iUniverse, 2007.

Gore, Albert. *An Inconvenient Truth: The Planetary Emergency of Global Warming and What We Can Do About It*. New York, NY: Rodale Books, 2006.

Gore, Albert. *Our Choice: How We Can Solve the Climate Crisis*. New York, NY: Puffin Books, 2009.

Gray, Kenneth. *Getting Real: Helping Teens Find Their Future*. 2nd ed. Thousand Oaks, CA: Corwin Press, 2009.

Hood, Beth, and Jim Hood. *Test Drive Your Future, High School Student and Grad Edition: Your Step by Step Guide to Choosing the Perfect Career*. Kamuela, HI: A Little Bit More Fun, Inc., 2010.

Llewellyn, A. Bronwyn. *The Everything Career Tests Book: 10 Tests to Determine the Right Occupation for You*. Avon, MA: F+W Publications, 2007.

Llewellyn, A. Bronwyn. *Green Jobs: A Guide to Eco-Friendly Employment*. Avon, MA: Adams Media and F+W Publications, 2008.

Lore, Nicholas. *The Pathfinder: How to Choose or Change Your Career for a Lifetime of Satisfaction and Success*. New York, NY: Touchstone, 2012.

Moravek, Joseph. *HVACR 101*. Clifton Park, NY: Delmar Cengage Learning, 2008.

Nelson, Blake. *Destroy All Cars*. New York, NY: Scholastic Paperbacks, 2011.

Nemko, Marty, and Richard Bolles. *Cool Careers for Dummies*. 3rd ed. Hoboken, NJ: Wiley Publishing, 2007.

Savedge, Jenn. *The Green Teen: The Eco-friendly Teen's Guide to Saving the Planet*. Gabriola Island, BC, Canada: New Society Publishers, 2009.

Schuster, R.J. *No Ducks in the Attic: & Other Basics of HVAC Installation*. Charleston, SC: Booksurge Publishing, 2009.

Silberstein, Eugene. *Residential Construction Academy HVAC*. 2nd ed. Clifton Park, NY: Delmar Cengage Learning, 2011.

Silvertsen, Linda, and Tosh Silvertsen. *Generation Green: The Ultimate Teen Guide to Living an Eco-friendly Life*. New York, NY: Simon Pulse, 2008.

Tieger, Paul, and Barbara Barron-Tieger. *Do What You Are: Discover the Perfect Career for You Through the Secrets of Personality Type*. 4th ed. New York, NY: Little, Brown and Company, 2007.

bibliography

American School Search. "HVAC Schools." Retrieved July 7, 2012 (http://www.american-school-search.com/colleges /hvac).

Brain, Marshall. *A Teenager's Guide to the Real World*. Raleigh, NC: BYG Publishing, 1997.

Bureau of Labor Statistics. "Heating, Air Conditioning and Refrigeration Mechanics and Installers." U.S. Department of Labor, 2012. Retrieved April 27, 2012 (http://www.bls .gov/ooh).

CollegeScholarships.org. "HVAC Scholarship Programs." 2012. Retrieved May 7, 2012 (http://www.collegescholarships.org /scholarships/hvac-students.htm).

Contracting Business. "Career Day Brings the World of HVAC to 400 Ninth-Graders." March 1, 2003. Retrieved April 29, 2012 (http://www.contractingbusiness.com /news/cb_imp_5530).

Eastland-Fairfield Career and Technical Schools. "College Tech Prep Program-Fairfield Career Center." 2012. Retrieved May 7, 2012 (http://www.eastland-fairfield. com/HighSchool/programs/aspx).

Fey, Carol. "Energy Is Put to Good Use in Antarctica." Mechanical Contracting, July 7, 2009. Retrieved July 21, 2012 (http://contractormag.com/plumbing_heating_and _cooling/energy-good-use-antarctica-0709).

Green Foot Steps. "Magnetic Refrigeration—The New Eco-friendly Way to Keep Things Cool." 2012. Retrieved May 5, 2012 (http://www.greenfootsteps.com/magnetic -refrigeration.html).

Leamy, Elisabeth. "The Indoor Pollution Threat You May Not Have Known Existed." ABC News Blogs, January 19,

2012. Retrieved July 29, 2012 (http://abcnews.go.com /blogs/health/2012/01/19).

Manchester Community College. "Associate Degree Curriculum: Heating, Ventilation, and Air Conditioning." 2012. Retrieved June 20, 2012 (http://www.mccnh .edu/academics/programs/heating-ventilation-and-air-conditioning).

Martynes, Shivaun. "Exploring HVAC Careers Part 2: The Best Entry Level HVAC Jobs." IntelliTec College, December 23, 2011. Retrieved July 18, 2012 (http://www .intelliteccollege.com/blog/556).

McCay, Dawn Rosenburg. "HVAC Technician Quiz." 2012. Retrieved May 13, 2012 (http://www.careerplanning.about .com/library/quiz/career_quizzes/blhvactechquiz/htm).

Michel, Matt. "NATE Impact Study." Service Roundtable, September 2006. Retrieved May 8, 2012 (http://www .serviceroundtable.com/freebies/viewfreebie/asp?PCID=1469).

Music with Ease. "Fats Domino Quotes." Retrieved August 2, 2012 (http://www.musicwithease.com/fats-domino -quotes.html).

National Center for Healthy Housing. "A New Prescription for Asthma Sufferers: Healthier Homes." Retrieved May 6, 2012 (http://www.nchh.org/Portal/0/contents/breath_easy_r2.pdf).

Pabst, Georgia. "New Job Corps Center Prepares Youths for Careers." *Milwaukee Journal Sentinel*, June 27, 2011. Retrieved May 15, 2012 (http://www.jsonline.com/news /milwaukee/12469293.html).

Plumbing, Heating, Cooling Contractors Association of Iowa. "2011–2012 Statewide License Compliant Plumbing and HVAC Apprenticeship Programs." 2011. Retrieved May 7, 2012 (http://www.phccia.org/images/stories/Apprenticeship Brochure-Pgformat.pdf).

Rosen, Rebecca. "Data Furnaces: The HVAC System of the Future." *Atlantic*, July 2011. Retrieved May 17, 2012 (http://www.theatlantic.com/technology/archive/2011/07/data-furnaces-the-hvac-system-of-the-future/242613).

Shatkin, Laurence. *Best Jobs for the 21st Century.* 6th ed. St. Paul, MN: JIST Publishing, 2012.

SkillsUSA. "SkillsUSA Fact Sheet." Retrieved May 13, 2012 (http://www.skillsusa.org/about/factsheet.shtml).

Snyder, Allen (energy manager [retired], Harrah's Resourt and Casino, Las Vegas, Nevada). Interview with the author, June 8, 2012.

U.S. Congress Joint Economic Committee. "Women and the Economy 2010: 25 Years of Progress but Challenges Remain." August 2010. Retrieved June 25, 2012 (http://www.jec.senate.gov/public/index.cfm?p=Reports1&ContentRecord_id=f5b62c08-227f-42b2-89d5-886a60f22131).

index

ABOUT THE AUTHOR

Linda Bickerstaff firmly believes that a four-year liberal arts education is not for everyone. In her book *Cool Careers Without College for People Who Love to Fix Things*, she featured a chapter on the HVAC industry. She welcomed the chance to expand her knowledge of the profession while doing the research for this topic. A career in HVAC is a very good choice for young people who prefer hands-on jobs that provide a very real sense of accomplishment at the end of the day.

PHOTO CREDITS

Cover Dmitry Kalinovsky/Shutterstock.com; cover (background), p. 3 Tony Weller/Photodisc/Getty Images; p. 4 Joe Raedle/Getty Images; pp. 8–9, 15, 45 © Trane; p. 11 MedicalRF.com/Getty Images; p. 17 Bloomberg/Getty Images; pp. 20–21 © AP Images; pp. 24–25 www.HVACRedu.net; pp. 26–27, 40–41, 48–49 © Peter Magallanes of HVAC Technical Institute; pp. 30–31 © Jim West/PhotoEdit; p. 32 Joseph Morrill; p. 35 Airman 1st Class Kate Thornston-Mauer/DVIDS; p. 43 courtesy and copyright of HVAC Excellence; p. 51 Plumbers & Steamfitters Local Union 21; p. 53 Craig Cozart/E+/Getty Images; pp. 56–57 Hill Street Studios/Blend Images/Getty Images; pp. 60–61 Kaehler, Wolfgang/SuperStock; p. 64 Noah Clayton/Photodisc/Getty Images.

Designer: Brian Garvey; Editor: Kathy Kuhtz Campbell; Photo Researcher: Marty Levick